Christine O'Brien

THE
Norton Anthology OF American Literature

Shorter Edition

1382
x

1427

Early American Literature 1620–1820 · MURPHY

American Literature 1820–1865 · PARKER

American Literature 1865–1914 · GOTTESMAN

American Literature between the Wars 1914–1945 · HOLLAND

Contemporary American Prose 1945– · PRITCHARD

Contemporary American Poetry 1945– · KALSTONE

Preface

THIS SHORTER EDITION of *The Norton Anthology of American Literature* has been prepared for the convenience of teachers who wish to have all the materials for a course within the covers of a single volume. The book, distilled from the rich resources of the parent volume, is designed to serve either a short course in American literature or else a longer course in which a "core" anthology is to be supplemented by a number of individual texts. Teachers of both types of course will find in this Shorter Edition the essential authors and selections, from the earliest years to the present, that they wish to teach, together with a useful reorganization of the materials and succinct and up-to-date editorial aids necessary for an adequate understanding of the text.

All sections of the anthology have been freshly conceived. We have dropped the traditional period names and have discontinued the practice of organizing writers according to "influences" and "schools." In our simplified arrangement, we merely assign time-span titles to the six sections into which the book is divided, and with very few exceptions, we arrange all the authors chronologically by date of birth. This change eliminates period labels, group labels, and topic labels that encourage students to prejudge the literature, and permits teachers the utmost flexibility in organizing their own courses. Thus—to single out the most important instance—Whitman and Dickinson simply appear in their appropriate chronological places in the section entitled "American Literature 1820–1865."

One of the most important innovations is that the editors have, for the first time, given proper attention to the diverse and significant achievements of recent American writing. They have, therefore, subdivided the usual standard but amorphous category "twentieth-century literature." The section "American Literature between the Wars 1914–1945" recognizes that these three decades are a definable literary span with its own literary history. The body of literature since World War II has, in its turn, been divided into separate sections of prose and poetry. This division has enabled the editors to write introductions and other editorial aids as well as to make their selections in such a way as to assist students in understanding the movements, trends, and careers in contemporary prose

But now amongst his company there was far another kind of carriage in this misery than amongst the passengers. For they that before had been boon companions in drinking and jollity in the time of their health and welfare, began now to desert one another in this calamity, saying they would not hazard their lives for them, they should be infected by coming to help them in their cabins; and so, after they came to lie by it, would do little or nothing for them but, "if they died, let them die." But such of the passengers as were yet aboard showed them what mercy they could, which made some of their hearts relent, as the boatswain (and some others) who was a proud young man and would often curse and scoff at the passengers. But when he grew weak, they had compassion on him and helped him; then he confessed he did not deserve it at their hands, he had abused them in word and deed. "Oh!" (saith he) "you, I now see, show your love like Christians indeed one to another, but we let one another lie and die like dogs." Another lay cursing his wife, saying if it had not been for her he had never come this unlucky voyage, and anon cursing his fellows, saying he had done this and that for some of them; he had spent so much and so much amongst them, and they were now weary of him and did not help him, having need. Another gave his companion all he had, if he died, to help him in his weakness; he went and got a little spice and made him a mess of meat once or twice. And because he died not so soon as he expected, he went amongst his fellows and swore the rogue would cozen[1] him, he would see him choked before he made him any more meat; and yet the poor fellow died before morning.

From *Book II, Chapter XXIII. Anno Dom: 1632*

[PROSPERITY BRINGS DISPERSAL OF POPULATION]

Also the people of the Plantation began to grow in their outward estates, by reason of the flowing of many people into the country, especially into the Bay of the Massachusetts. By which means corn and cattle rose to a great price, by which many were much enriched and commodities grew plentiful. And yet in other regards this benefit turned to their hurt, and this accession of strength to their weakness. For now as their stocks increased and the increase vendible,[2] there was no longer any holding them together, but now they must of necessity go to their great lots. They could not otherwise keep their cattle, and having oxen grown they must have land for plowing and tillage. And no man now thought he could live except he had cattle and a great deal of ground to keep them, all striving to increase their stocks. By which means they were scattered all over the Bay quickly and the town in which they lived compactly till now was left very thin and in a short time almost desolate.

And if this had been all, it had been less, though too much; but

1. Cheat.

2. Salable.

and carriages in other; but they were soon quelled and overcome by the wisdom, patience, and just and equal carriage of things, by the Governor and better part, which clave[6] faithfully together in the main.

[THE STARVING TIME]

But that which was most sad and lamentable was, that in two or three months' time half of their company died, especially in January and February, being the depth of winter, and wanting houses and other comforts; being infected with the scurvy and other diseases which this long voyage and their inaccommodate condition had brought upon them. So as there died some times two or three of a day in the foresaid time, that of 100 and odd persons, scarce fifty remained. And of these, in the time of most distress, there was but six or seven persons who to their great commendations, be it spoken, spared no pains night nor day, but with abundance of toil and hazard of their own health, fetched them wood, made them fires, dressed them meat, made their beds, washed their loathsome clothes, clothed and unclothed them. In a word, did all the homely[7] and necessary offices for them which dainty and queasy stomachs cannot endure to hear named; and all this willingly and cheerfully, without any grudging in the least, showing herein their true love unto their friends and brethren; a rare example and worthy to be remembered. Two of these seven were Mr. William Brewster, their reverend Elder, and Myles Standish, their Captain and military commander, unto whom myself and many others were much beholden in our low and sick condition. And yet the Lord so upheld these persons as in this general calamity they were not at all infected either with sickness or lameness. And what I have said of these I may say of many others who died in this general visitation, and others yet living; that whilst they had health, yea, or any strength continuing, they were not wanting[8] to any that had need of them. And I doubt not but their recompense is with the Lord.

But I may not here pass by another remarkable passage not to be forgotten. As this calamity fell among the passengers that were to be left here to plant, and were hasted ashore and made to drink water that the seamen might have the more beer, and one[9] in his sickness desiring but a small can of beer, it was answered that if he were their own father he should have none. The disease began to fall amongst them also, so as almost half of their company died before they went away, and many of their officers and lustiest men, as the boatswain, gunner, three quartermasters, the cook and others. At which the Master was something strucken and sent to the sick ashore and told the Governor he should send for beer for them that had need of it, though he drunk water homeward bound.

6. Past tense of *cleave*.
7. Intimate.
8. Lacking in attention.
9. "Which was this author himself" [Bradford's note].

If I worship one thing more than another it shall be the spread of
my own body, or any part of it,
Translucent mould of me it shall be you!
Shaded ledges and rests it shall be you!
Firm masculine colter[4] it shall be you!
Whatever goes to the tilth[5] of me it shall be you!
You my rich blood! your milky stream pale strippings of my life!
Breast that presses against other breasts it shall be you!
My brain it shall be your occult convolutions!
Root of wash'd sweet-flag! timorous pond-snipe! nest of guarded
duplicate eggs! it shall be you!
Mix'd tussled hay of head, beard, brawn, it shall be you!
Trickling sap of maple, fibre of manly wheat, it shall be you!
Sun so generous it shall be you!
Vapors lighting and shading my face it shall be you!
You sweaty brooks and dews it shall be you!
Winds whose soft-tickling genitals rub against me it shall be you!
Broad muscular fields, branches of live oak, loving lounger in my
winding paths, it shall be you!
Hands I have taken, face I have kiss'd, mortal I have ever touch'd,
it shall be you.

I dote on myself, there is that lot of me and all so luscious,
Each moment and whatever happens thrills me with joy,
I cannot tell how my ankles bend, nor whence the cause of my
faintest wish,
Nor the cause of the friendship I emit, nor the cause of the friend-
ship I take again.

That I walk up my stoop, I pause to consider if it really be,
A morning-glory at my window satisfies me more than the meta-
physics of books.

To behold the day-break!
The little light fades the immense and diaphanous shadows,
The air tastes good to my palate.

Hefts[6] of the moving world at innocent gambols silently rising
freshly exuding,
Scooting obliquely high and low.

Something I cannot see puts upward libidinous prongs,
Seas of bright juice suffuse heaven.

The earth by the sky staid with, the daily close of their junction,
The heav'd challenge from the east that moment over my head,
The mocking taunt, See then whether you shall be master!

4. This phallic passage begins with reference to the blade at the front of a plow.
5. Plowing; here, any cultivation or personal improvement.
6. Something being heaved or raised upward.

24

Walt Whitman, a kosmos, of Manhattan the son,
Turbulent, fleshy, sensual, eating, drinking and breeding,
No sentimentalist, no stander above men and women or apart from them,
No more modest than immodest.

Unscrew the locks from the doors!
Unscrew the doors themselves from their jambs!

Whoever degrades another degrades me,
And whatever is done or said returns at last to me.

Through me the afflatus[3] surging and surging, through me the current and index.

I speak the pass-word primeval, I give the sign of democracy,
By God! I will accept nothing which all cannot have their counterpart of on the same terms.

Through me many long dumb voices,
Voices of the interminable generations of prisoners and slaves,
Voices of the diseas'd and despairing and of thieves and dwarfs,
Voices of cycles of preparation and accretion,
And of the threads that connect the stars, and of wombs and of the father-stuff,
And of the rights of them the others are down upon,
Of the deform'd, trivial, flat, foolish, despised,
Fog in the air, beetles rolling balls of dung.

Through me forbidden voices,
Voices of sexes and lusts, voices veil'd and I remove the veil,
Voices indecent by me clarified and transfigur'd.

I do not press my fingers across my mouth,
I keep as delicate around the bowels as around the head and heart,
Copulation is no more rank to me than death is.

I believe in the flesh and the appetites,
Seeing, hearing, feeling, are miracles, and each part and tag of me is a miracle.

Divine am I inside and out, and I make holy whatever I touch or am touch'd from,
The scent of these arm-pits aroma finer than prayer,
This head more than churches, bibles, and all the creeds.

3. Divine wind or spirit.